We would like to tell you something about John Byrne, but all we can say is that he is a cartoonist and comedy writer who has written lots of successful joke books and turns up on TV quite a bit. To reveal anything else would put him in serious danger. (Not from enemy spies, but from his mum, who thinks he works in a bank.)

The World's DEADLIEST joke book!

John Byrne

PUFFIN BOOKS

PUFFIN BOOKS

Published by the Penguin Group
Penguin Books Ltd, 80 Strand, London WC2R 0RL, England
Penguin Putnam Inc., 375 Hudson Street, New York, New York 10014, USA
Penguin Books Australia Ltd, 250 Camberwell Road, Camberwell, Victoria 3124, Australia
Penguin Books Canada Ltd, 10 Alcorn Avenue, Toronto, Ontario, Canada M4V 3B2
Penguin Books India (P) Ltd, 11 Community Centre, Panchsheel Park, New Delhi – 110 017, India
Penguin Books (NZ) Ltd, Cnr Rosedale and Airborne Roads, Albany, Auckland, New Zealand
Penguin Books (South Africa) (Pty) Ltd, 24 Sturdee Avenue, Rosebank 2196, South Africa

www.penguin.com

Penguin Books Ltd, Registered Offices: 80 Strand, London WC2R 0RL, England

First published 2002
1

Made and printed in England by Clays Ltd, St Ives plc

British Library Cataloguing in Publication Data
A CIP catalogue record for this book is available from the British Library

ISBN 0-141-31359-5

WELCOME TO
THE WORLD'S DEADLIEST JOKE BOOK

It's full of ... well, with so many spies, double agents and other doers of dastardly deeds knocking around, I'd better not tell you what it's about. What I will say is that we've wired every page of this book with a secret camera and if we catch you telling anyone what's in here, we'll be straight round to wipe that silly grin off your face. What do you mean, that's not a silly grin, that's your normal expression?

Well, never mind, there's lots of information here on camouflage, disguise and other essential secret skills. And of course, as it's the world's *deadliest* joke book, we've put in lots of jokes to make you die laughing (or at least you'll be dying to send better jokes in for our next book).

OK – it's time to start reading, and don't forget this book will self-destruct in five seconds. Er, hang on, I seem to have got the wires crossed.

Looks like the book is going to stay around a bit longer and I'M going to self-destruct in five seconds ... four ... three ... two ...

Bernard Boom
Ex-Principal
St Sneaky's School for Spies

BADDIE BONANZA

WHEN DOES THE GOVERNMENT CALL IN VAMPIRE SPIES?

Who's the world's deadliest underwear model?
The Wicked Witch of the Vest.

ONLY WHEN THE COUNTRY IS UNDER GRAVE THREAT.

RIP

Who's the world's deadliest bird watcher?
Count Duckula.

WHY ARE
TORTOISES
GOOD AT
REMEMBERING
CODES?

Who's the world's
deadliest baker?
Attila the Bun.

BECAUSE WE
HAVE
TURTLE
RECALL.

Who's the world's
deadliest tortoise?
Ivan the Terrapin.

Who's the world's deadliest
bow-tie maker?
The Sheriff of Knotting'em

Who's the world's deadliest
mime artist?
*Hey, you forgot to put an answer
to that joke!*
*No, we didn't – that was a deadly
silence!*

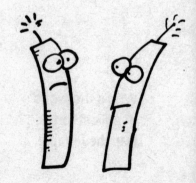

Who's the world's
deadliest fishmonger?
Jack the Kipper.

Who's the world's
deadliest movie star?
Brad Pitt-Bull.

WHAT DO YOU
DO TO PEOPLE
WHO DON'T LAUGH
AT DEADLY
DOG
JOKES?

I RUFF THEM
UP...

Who's the world's deadliest
indoor games player?
Darts Vader.

SPY SCHOOL ENTRANCE EXAM

1 **Have you wanted to be a spy since you were very young?**

a. Yes

b. No

c. How should I know? Since I became a spy I've been brainwashed and given a whole new identity.

WHY DO YOU KEEP SHINING IN MY EYES?

IN CASE YOU GET ANY BRIGHT IDEAS!

2 **Are you incredibly brave and tough?**

a. Yes

b. No

c. Wahhh! Don't bother me now – I've got this really nasty paper cut from turning the pages in this book.

3 **Code-breaking test: If the first three letters in a sequence are T-Z-H, which letter comes next?**

a. The letter Y

b. The letter X

c. The letter I send asking my mate Agent 006 to help me out – she's really good at codes.

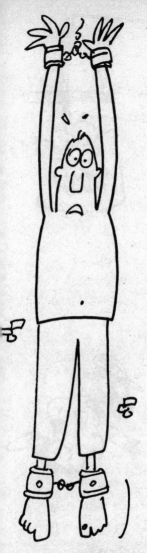

STUDYING FOR THIS TEST REALLY HAS ME OVERSTRETCHED!

4 Are you good at handling top-secret gadgets?

a. Yes

b. No

c. I'll have to come back to this question – my pen's just turned into a bazooka and I can't work out how to change it back.

5 Would you give away secrets if you were horribly tortured?

a. Yes

b. No

c. I'm not going to tell you, no matter what you do.

6 Are you prepared to die for your country?

a. Yes

b. No

c. Of course I am – what colour would you like me to dye myself?

7 Can you beat up a huge enemy attacker with one hand tied behind your back?

a. Yes

b. No

c. Maybe – but I'd prefer it if you tied both of *his* hands behind *his* back.

8 **Will you ever become a double agent and sell our secrets to the Other Side?**

a. Yes
b. Of course I won't.
c. What was the question again? I was busy talking to my contact on the Other Side.

HOW DID YOU SCORE?
What does it matter? Any self-respecting spy will already have a fake copy of the diploma.

HOW DID YOU DO IN YOUR EXPLOSIVES EXAM?

WHOOOM!

I BOMBED!

Spies! Have YOU been foiled by a faulty
fake nose? Have you ever wept over a wonky wig?
Cut-price camouflage is a thing of the past with:

Disguise the Limit!

Buy a disguise from us and it is guaranteed to be one
hundred per cent lifelike or we'll give you your money back!*

*Your disguise will be one hundred per cent lifelike because we'll make it look exactly like YOU.
And don't hold your breath while waiting for your money back – we've already put on the disguise
that looks like you and have taken out all of the money from your bank account.

DEADLY
JOKE FILE #1

First Spy: oohsitA!
Second Spy: Don't you mean 'Atishoo'?
First Spy: Yes, but I've got a code in my nose!

WHY ARE YOU WEARING YOUR COMPUTER?

COS I HEARD SPIES WERE SUPPOSED TO DRESS IN A MACINTOSH!

Why did the spy hit his computer with a hammer?
He was trying to break the codes.

What musical instrument
do secret agents play?
The spy-olin.

WHY ARE
MUSICAL SPIES
EASY TO GET RID OF?

CLUNK!

What musical instrument
do counterfeiters play?
The fiddle.

COS THEY MAKE
GREAT GUITAR-GETS!

Whack!

What musical instrument do telephone
surveillance experts play?
They don't – they just tap their toes.

How do skunks defend
themselves?
With pong fu.

HAiiii!!
NOW THAT'S WHAT
I CALL "KICKING
UP A STINK!"

Why do ninjas carry
sticking plasters?
To tend to their ninja-ries.

What do you call a secret
agent on drums?
James Bongo.

WHAT TYPE
OF DRUM ARE
YOU?

I'M NOT
TELLING
YOU. YOU'LL
HAVE TO
BEAT IT
OUT OF ME!

Where do you get cheap
ejector seats?
In the spring sales.

ASK AGENT AGONY

Are you a scared spy or an anxious assassin?

Don't despair, send your problems to Agent Agony. Remember, the writer of each month's star letter gets £1,000.*

*That's not the prize – that's the price on their head for revealing official secrets.

Dear Agent Agony

Can you give me some advice on self-defence?

Threatened, Twickenham

Dear Threatened

The best advice I can give you on self-defence is don't attack yourself in the first place.

HOW DO SKUNKS WRITE LETTERS?
WITH INVISIBLE STINK!

Dear Agent Agony

Can you give me any tips on becoming a sharpshooter?

Eagle Eye, East Ham

Dear Eagle Eye

Certainly – before you start shooting, put the barrel of your gun into a pencil sharpener.

WHY DON'T YOU — WRITE TO AGENT AGONY?

'COS YOU'RE ALWAYS TELLING ME NOT TO SHOOT MY MOUTH OFF!'

Dear Agent Agony

You've got to help me! Someone has just slipped a pellet of deadly poison into my drink!

If you don't send me an antidote, I have been told that it will slowly creep through my system and in just twenty-seven days from now, I will be dead!

Panicky, Penge

Dear Panicky

Don't worry – I have put the antidote in the post just this minute.

PS Please allow twenty-eight days for delivery.

Dear Agent Agony

Thank you for sending a personal reply to my recent letter. Unfortunately, I couldn't read it as the page was blank. Did you write it in invisible ink?

Suspicious, Surrey

Dear Suspicious

No – it's just that I can't use my pencil because there's a gun stuck in my pencil sharpener.

Dear Agent Agony

Because he cuts the letters out of the newspaper while I am still READING it!

Really Worried, Secret Location*

*Moved from Worcester because I was scared.

Dear Agent Agony

Somebody has been cutting letters out of the newspaper and using them to send me threatening notes. This is really upsetting me and I am scared that they are from a really tough supervillain.

Worried, Worcester

Dear Worried

Huh! Some secret agent YOU are – lots of people get threatening notes with letters cut out from the newspaper. What makes you think these ones are from a really tough supervillain?

Dear Agent Agony

As I am a top-secret secret agent, I have sent my problem to you on the enclosed tape. It will self-destruct five minutes after you have listened to it. I hope you will be able to give me some advice.

Sneaky, Siberia

Dear Sneaky

My advice to you is that your watch is five minutes slow. The tape self-destructed as soon as I opened the envelo

Dear Agent Agony

I am a top-secret agent with a problem - my day-to-day life is so full of explosions, adventures and death-defying stunts that when I take a holiday, I find it really boring. What can I do?

Daring, Dorset

Dear Daring

Zzzzzzzzzzz ... sorry, you were going on about your exciting life so much, you bored me to sleep.

MYSTERIOUS MIRTH

Who is the naughtiest secret
agent in spy school?
Trouble-O-Seven.

What do you get if you cross a
secret agent with Jack and the
Beanstalk?
Fee-Spy-Fo-Fum!

SPECIAL OFFER!

ONE HUNDRED PER CENT ABSOLUTELY FOOLPROOF GUARANTEED REALISTIC FAKE ID

No tricks, no gimmicks – this is quite simply the most realistic fake ID in the whole spying world. Send us your cheque for £1,000 and we'll send your ID by return of post.*

*On second thoughts, we'll probably hang on to your money, and your purchase too. I mean, with all these fake IDs floating around, how do we know if you really are who you say you are?

19

When your life is full of danger, who wants a toy that does the same thing?

Now there's a fully posable* figure especially designed for the resting agent ...

INACTION MAN!

*Fully posable, that is, if the poses you have in mind are 'sleeping', 'slumped in front of the TV' and, our special favourite, 'hiding at the slightest hint of danger'.

And once you've got your own Inaction Man figure, you'll also want these really unexciting accessories:

INACTION MAN game of bowls
INACTION MAN flower-arranging set
INACTION MAN reads a John Byrne joke book*

*Comes complete with electronic snoring sounds.

Send your order for INACTION MAN today – but don't expect us to do anything about it.

SECRET SNIGGERS

What did the spy say when he
left his watch on his ejector seat?
'Gosh, how time flies!'

What do you get if you cross
a gorilla with a famous spy?
Mata Hairy.

CAMOUFLAGE CONUNDRUM!

Agent D. Deadly, master of disguise, is hiding somewhere on these pages. Take a close look and see if you can find him.

Why does Dr Evil like having a cat on his lap?
So he can keep up with the latest mews.

WHAT'S GREEN AND DANGEROUS AND HAS SPOTS AND BAD TEETH?

What do posh crocodiles use when they're eating you?
Snap-kins.

A CHOCO-DILE!

What sneaks up behind cavemen and blows a trumpet in their ear?
A sabre-toot tiger.

Which creatures make
the best secret agents?
Spyders.

HOW DO SNAKES
FIND OUT
SECRETS?
BY BEING
CHARMING.

Why do ducks
make such good
spies?
**They are great at
quacking codes.**

What did the mummy
cobra say to the baby
cobra?
**'It's raining – put up your
hood.'**

What has a mane, a
cowboy hat and a large
country music collection?
A lion dancer.

How did the bull leave the
bullring?
Straight through the matador.

MARTIAL ARTS
MADNESS

What do you get if you cross a candlestick maker with a black belt?
I don't know, but if he's got a black belt, I'd be very careful not to get on his wick!

WHAT DO YOU FIND AT A BUSY MARTIAL ARTS CLASS?

What did the plank of wood say after the karate class?
'I'm absolutely shattered!'

A KUNG QUEUE.

How do kung fu instructors buy their equipment?
On hi-yah purchase.

Why do martial arts experts
wear black belts?
To keep their trousers up.

WHY DID THE SNAKE
LOSE ALL HIS KUNG FU
TOURNAMENTS?

Why couldn't the martial arts
teacher come to class?
He had kung flu.

What do you get if you cross
a butcher with a black belt?
Karate chops.

BECAUSE
HIS BLOWS
WERE
ARMLESS.

What do you get if you cross
a baker with a black belt?
Ju-dough.

The DEADLY ART of JOKE FU

BREATHING:

Breathing techniques are a very important part of the martial arts. Many great masters have spent years mastering their breathing. You might not think that this would be very useful when you are in deadly danger, but study the two examples here and you'll see just how important it can be:

LESSON ONE

Martial Arts Breathing Method (Traditional Version)

1. The student spends many years learning to control their breathing.

2. In a dangerous situation, the student uses controlled breathing to produce a state of great relaxation, which will help them make the best use of their martial arts skills.

3. Unfortunately, if the student has spent too many years studying breathing, they get so relaxed they fall asleep, allowing the mugger to nick their stuff without even thumping them first.

Martial Arts Breathing Method (Joke Fu Version)

1. Student doesn't spend many years studying breathing. Instead, student spends most of pocket money on garlic, mature cheese and those pickled-onion-flavour crisps.

2. When mugger strikes, student merely breathes normally.

3. Trust us – with that pongy breath, the mugger won't be doing any breathing for quite some time!

SHOUTING:

Shouting techniques are another very important part of the martial arts. We said, 'SHOUTING TECHNIQUES ARE ANOTHER VERY IMPORTANT PART OF THE MARTIAL ARTS!'

When a great master shouts loudly, they channel all of the energy in their body so that they can attack their opponent at their weakest point (which, with all that shouting going on, is likely to be their eardrums).

LESSON TWO

Martial Arts Shouting Method (Traditional Version)

1. When danger strikes, the student shouts very loudly and uses the energy released to shatter a concrete block with their bare hands.

2. The attacker falls to the ground trembling.

Martial Arts Shouting Method (Joke Fu Version)

1. When danger strikes, student does exactly the same as above ... just in a different order. First comes the shattering of the concrete block with bare hands, then comes the loud shout. This is because it is actually your bare hands that are shattering.

2. Attacker will still fall to the ground trembling – only this time it will be with laughter.

MEDITATION:

In order to get your mind and body working together, you've got to practise meditation. Meditating means you forget about the cares and distractions of the everyday world and just let your mind drift away. What do you mean, you've been doing meditation in the back of your Maths class for years?

Martial Arts Meditation Method (Traditional Version)

1. The student must first sit in a special position called the lotus position.

2. The student makes one long, continuous sound called a mantra and clears the mind of all thoughts.

3. The student achieves inner peace.

Martial Arts Meditation Method (Joke Fu Version)

1. Student sits in lotus position.

2. Student makes one long, continuous sound and clears mind of all thoughts (except for 'wish I hadn't had that curry for lunch').

3. Student achieves inner peace. Also, outer peace. Mostly because student is now so knotted up in lotus position, it's impossible to get out and meet anyone.

THROWING:

Masters of the Secret Art of Joke Fu only pick fights with
the biggest, toughest opponents. (Which explains why there
are so few Joke Fu masters left around and why the art is
such a secret.)

LESSON FOUR

Martial Arts Throwing (Joke Fu Version)

1. When attacker strikes, the student throws him/herself on the ground and begs for mercy.

2. Attacker has a good laugh at wimpy martial artist and throws a party for his mates so that they can have a good laugh too.

3. Student throws switch on remote-controlled crane hidden around corner.

4. Student tosses joke fu manual in the bin as attacker and mates have been sent to prison and they've thrown away the key.

Martial Arts Throwing (Traditional Version)

1. When attacker strikes, the student gets a firm grip on their arm and throws them over his/her shoulder.

SPY SCHOOL RULES:

No running in the corridors unless being chased by deadly enemies.
(Please note – if the deadly enemy in question is one of your teachers, this doesn't count.)

Pupils must not wear school uniform at any time. (This is so that we can distinguish pupils from our Disguise teachers, who will, of course, have turned up wearing school uniforms as a disguise.)

3 Pupils are forbidden to break into the headmaster's office and secretly copy the answers to the end-of-term exam.

If any pupil HAS broken into the headmaster's office and secretly copied the answers to the end-of term exam, could they please tell the headmaster as he's lost his own copy.

Could pupils please stop submitting essays on microfilm as it's ruining the teachers' eyes.

> You at the back, sit up straight – our eyes aren't that bad just yet.

> There will be no talking in class – especially not on those tiny hidden microphones.

> We said, 'THERE WILL BE NO TALKING IN CLASS!' You really need to get new batteries for your tiny hidden microphone.

9 Pupils must be polite to teachers at all times. And don't try telling us that 'Baldy Old Trout' is actually secret code for 'O Respected Educator' because we've heard that one before.

10 Please make sure you remove any hidden cameras from the inside of an apple before giving it to the teacher. If you forget to do this and the teacher swallows it, something terrible might develop.

11 Pupils may have the rest of the year off.

12 Actually, Rule 11 translates as: Pupils will be given double homework for the rest of the year. See? We Baldy Old Trouts can play around with codes too!

NAiL-BiTiNG NONSeNSe

Writer One: My new thriller is full of suspense.
Writer Two: **What's it about?**
Writer One: I'll tell you tomorrow.

WHY DO
ELEPHANTS
MAKE REALLY
GOOD SECRET
AGENTS?

What does Harrison
Ford feed his dog?
Indiana Bones.

BECAUSE
WE'VE ALWAYS
GOT THE
ELE-MENT
OF
SURPRISE!

How does Indiana Jones find
things in the jungle?
With Radars of the Lost Ark.

'Waiter, there's a thriller novel in my breakfast bowl!'
'Don't worry, sir – it's part of a serial.'

WHAT DID ONE
PARACHUTE JUMPER
SAY TO THE OTHER
PARACHUTE JUMPER?

TWO'S COMPANY,
THREE'S A
CLOUD!

What do stuntmen wear to keep warm?
Parachute jumpers.

How do snakes find out secrets? By being charming.

What did the boy spy say to the girl spy?
'Disguise in love with you ...'

G-get involved in s-spying?

N-no thanks.. I'm a yellowfants!

How do elephants spy on other elephants?
With an ele-scope.

DO PEOPLE SUSPECT THAT YOU ARE REALLY A SUPERSPY? ARE YOU BLOWING YOUR TOP IN FEAR THAT YOU'RE ABOUT TO BLOW YOUR COVER? KEEP YOUR SECRET SAFE WITH OUR SPECIALLY DESIGNED

SECRET SHIRT!

THE SECRET SHIRT COMES IN THREE SIZES:

- Small: Carrying the message: I am not a spy (as seen above).

- Large: Carrying the message: I am not a spy, nor am I a spy trying to put you off the scent by wearing a T-shirt saying I am not a spy.

- Extra-large: Carrying the message: I am not a spy, nor am I a spy trying to put you off the scent by wearing a T-shirt saying I am not a spy, nor am I a spy trying to put you off the scent by wearing a T-shirt saying I am not a spy.

Special Offer: With every extra-large T-shirt you get a free T-shirt saying, Oh, go on then, I am a spy. Because by the time people finish reading your other one, you'll have completed the entire five-year spying course.

When you're dicing with death or captured in a fiendish trap, it's easy to feel that you're all alone. (Well, OK. If the fiendish trap you're caught in happens to be a solitary confinement cell, you ARE all alone.) But a fiend in need is a fiend indeed, so forget your brilliant escape plan for a few minutes and draw some inspiration from the Experts in the Adventure Business.

TOUGH TALKING
WHERE HEROES DON'T HOLD BACK

OCCUPATION: SUPERHERO

What's your name?
The Mighty Mask.

And your real name?
It's A. Secret.

Oh, you mean your secret identity. We understand.
No – I mean it is A. Secret: Arthur Secret of 29 Toughguy
Terrace. I thought everyone knew that.

What are your superpowers?
Mighty Muscles, Incredible Stamina and er ... er ...

Superpower memory?
Oh, yeah. Thanks. I keep forgetting that one.

Are people amazed when they see you?
Yes, they always shout, 'Is it a bird? Is it a plane?'

When you fly through the air?
No, when I do my bird and plane impressions. Want to hear
one now?

Er, no thanks. Tell us about your greatest adventure.
Tell us about your greatest adventure.

We just said that.
I know – that was my parrot impression. Want to hear
another?

On second thoughts, we really must fly.
Lucky you. I've got to go everywhere by train and my cape
keeps getting caught in the doors. And thanks for not
printing my secret identity.

**No problem, Arthur Secret of 29 Toughguy Terrace. We'll see you
around.**

OCCUPATION: SECRET AGENT

What's your name?
007 and a Half.
Really? We were told it was 008.
I've been on a diet.
Have you got a licence to kill?
No, but I have got a licence to fill.
What does that mean?
I work as a petrol-pump attendant at night. This spying business doesn't pay very much, you know.
Aren't you afraid your enemies will recognize you when they drive into the petrol station?
Yes, but I usually manage to keep them fuelled.
Have you got any exciting secret-agent gadgets?
I've got a pen that turns into a pistol.
That's pretty cool.
Not really – I just shot a hole in my writing desk while I was doing this interview.
What's the scariest thing that ever happened to you?
I just shot a hole in my writing desk while I was filling out this questionnaire.
That's the same as your last answer.
I know, but my pistol is a repeater.
OK then, what's the scariest thing you think COULD happen to you?
That enemy agents will capture and completely brainwash me.
We're sure that will never happen, 008.
Who are you calling '008'? My name is Fido, I'm two years old and I am a giant banana. Now if you'll excuse me, I need to go and clear all this washing powder out of my head ...

OCCUPATION: LORD OF THE JUNGLE

What's your name?
Marzipan of the Apes.

Any relation to Tarzan?
He's my cousin, but I'm much sweeter.

Were you really raised by apes?
No, I was dropped by apes. After raising me for five minutes, their arms got tired.

You're famous for your ear-splitting yell ...
If you were dropped on your bottom by a load of apes, you'd yell too.

Why do you always swing through the jungle?
Because if I slid through the jungle, I'd do my bottom even more damage. Some of those leaves have very sharp edges.

Would you please stop talking about your bottom?
Sorry – that's what happens when you get raised by apes.

That must have been really hard for you.
Oh, it was OK. Except that the food drove me bananas.

Didn't you ask your ape mum to change your diet?
Yes, and then the food drove me nuts.

Is it true that you can talk to jungle animals and get them to obey your orders?
Ook ook ooky ook.

What on earth does that mean?
Don't ask me, mate. I'm a chimpanzee that Marzipan ordered to finish off this interview when he got bored doing it ...

OCCUPATION: SPACE EXPLORER

What's your name?
Captain Quirk.

What's the name of your ship?
The Starship Boobyprise.

Do you boldly go where no man has gone before?
Yes, I do.

That must be really scary!
Not really. No man went there before, but my mum and big sister have. They sent me a postcard.

Aren't you afraid there will be horrible-looking aliens out there?
There already are – you haven't seen my big sister.

So what ARE you scared of, then?
My big sister seeing my answer to the last question.

Been to any interesting planets?
Oh, yes – Planet Hollywood. They do really nice burgers.

No, we mean have you been out among the stars?
Well, the waiter at Planet Hollywood looked a bit like Harrison Ford ...

Why did you decide to become a space explorer anyway?
My Careers teacher said she could see I had the brain for it.

Were those her exact words?
Yes, she said, 'You've got a lot of space between your ears.'

We can see what she means. Any space trips planned at the moment?
No.

That's what you think.
What do you mean?

Your big sister's just read your answers to these questions and she says to get ready to disappear from the face of the earth.

OCCUPATION: WESTERN HERO

What's your name?
The Lonely Ranger.

What's the name of your horse?
Copper.

That's a funny name for a horse.
I know, but I couldn't afford one called 'Silver'.

Is it true that you're the fastest gun in the west?
No, I'm a bloke in a cowboy hat. The fastest gun is that
metal thing in my holster.

No, we meant are you quick on the draw?
I'm not as quick as that John Byrne guy. He's been drawing
cartoons all over this book.

But you can't strike terror into bad guys' hearts just by drawing.
I don't know about that. Some of John Byrne's drawings are
pretty terrible and if the cartoons don't terrorize you, the
awful jokes certainly will.

Have you ever stopped any hold-ups?
Sure have.

When was that?
Right now. I'm trying to get home for my tea and these
questions are holding me up.

What are you having for your tea?
Beans, like all cowboys do.

**OK – one last question. Why are you called 'The Lonely
Ranger'?**
Believe me, if YOU ate beans for breakfast, lunch and tea,
people wouldn't want to be around you either.

TOP SECRET TITTERS

Spy Teacher: Why have you got that
lamp on your head?
**Spy Pupil: You told me proper secret agents
always wear shades.**

WHY DO YOU INSIST ON
DOING YOUR HOMEWORK
WITH A LAMPSHADE ON
YOUR HEAD?

What's got six legs and
wears a disguise?
A secret age-ant.

I THOUGHT
IT MIGHT GIVE
ME SOME BRIGHT
IDEAS...

First Spy Teacher: Are all your
pupils good secret agents?
**Second Spy Teacher: Oh, yes. If
there's any good in them, they've
definitely kept it secret.**

What is the spy's favourite drink?
Code-a-Cola.

First Spy Teacher: I saw one of your pupils touching the electrified fence.
Second Spy Teacher: Don't worry – I'll make sure he's charged.

First Spy Pupil: Be careful what you say
– our teacher might be listening,
disguised as a tree . . .
**Second Spy Pupil: Don't worry, his
bark is worse than his bite.**

Where would you find lots of
animals with black belts?
In a kung zoo.

Available at last!

The amazing watch

every superagent needs!

You'll wonder how you ever got along without its special top-secret hidden feature!

Yes, we know high-tech watches are standard super-secret agent issue. You've already got a watch that cuts through sheet metal, a watch radio that links you to your secret headquarters by international satellite link-up and a watch that transforms into a fighter jet for those emergency escape situations, but after many requests from agents all over the world, we've come up with a watch that does something even more useful. Yes, believe it or not, this watch actually TELLS THE TIME! (Don't worry if it's been so long since you had a normal watch that you've forgotten how to tell the time, full instructions are enclosed.*)

*(For spies who have already ordered the watch and can't understand the instructions, please note that they are in plain English, so trying to decode them before you read them is only making life difficult.)

Send for your watch right away – please allow 28 days for delivery, or 48, or 2,007. Since you can't tell the time, what does it matter?

The Army pays thousands of pounds for them! No self-respecting super agent should be without them. And *The Deadliest Joke Book* is giving them to you, absolutely free. Turn the page for your

NIGHT-VISION GOGGLES!

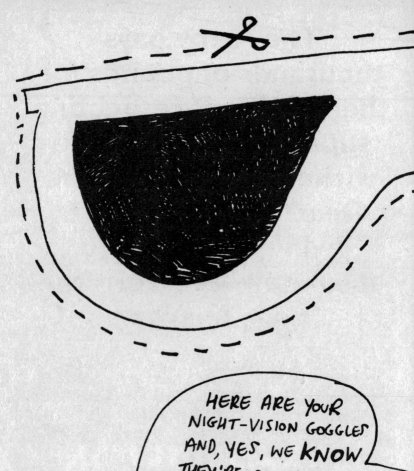

MAKE TRACKS

Before you venture out into
the unknown, 'paws' for a quick test that
might just save your life.
It's essential to be able to distinguish tracks left by big
nasty beasties from those left by cute little animals. A savage
lion, an angry gorilla and a cute little bunny rabbit have
passed this way quite recently. By looking at the prints on
this page, can you identify the bunny rabbit tracks and
follow them to safety?

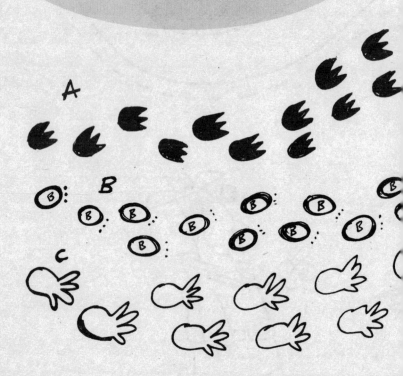

Not yourself today? Oh, you are. What a pity. Never mind – now you can get yourself out of any tricky situation with ...

The
ULTIMATE DISGUISE
Handbook!

The Ultimate Disguise Handbook will get you out of trouble because:

● It's got instructions for all the best disguises;

● It's written by a team of experts; and mostly because

● It's not actually a book at all. It's a fully functional nuclear warship *disguised* as a book.

Trust us – this is a book you won't be able to put down (simply because it's so heavy you won't be able to pick it up in the first place)!

SPY SCHOOL DINNER MENU

Starter:

Soup of the Day
(Please let us know in advance
if you would like deadly poison
slipped into your soup. And if
you do ask for deadly poison,
please DO NOT order the main
course, as it's a shame to see all that
food going to waste.)

WARNING:
All our school
dinner ladies are
licensed to kill. (Not with
weapons — with their
cooking.)

Main Course:

Alphabet Spaghetti (available coded or decoded)
Chicken and Chips (Please note: The chips are
microchips that one of our agents stole from the
enemy headquarters. The chicken is the same
agent who's hiding under your table as he's
scared the enemy is going to come after him and
thump him.)

Jacket Potatoes (all wearing bulletproof jackets)

Shark Surprise (a big surprise for you – the shark's still alive)

Side orders are also available.
(Note to Double Agents: Don't think you're going to get second helpings by changing sides halfway through the meal.)

YOU SAID YOU WANTED DINNER AND MAKE IT SNAPPY!

Dessert:

Baked Alaska (Please allow some time for this as our dinner ladies have to switch on the laser beam and aim it at Alaska.)
Gooseberry Fool (Actually a strawberry in disguise. Fooled you, didn't we?)

Drinks:

All drinks will be served shaken, not stirred. (Well, in a canteen like this one, you can't blame the staff for being nervous.)

Special Note for calorie-counters: Don't be afraid to order as much food as you like – you won't put on weight. After all, now that you've memorized the details of our menu, we'll have to kill you.

CLOCK THAT CREATURE!

In a deadly book like this one, it's really important to spot the most dangerous creature before it spots you. Test your survival skills by naming the most dangerous creature on these pages.

ANSWER:
If you said animal number 1, 2, 3, 4, 5, 7, 8 or 9, you are wrong. These so-called animals are, in fact, Agent D. Deadly, master of disguise, and his family on their annual trip to the zoo.

PS If you said animal number 6, you are also wrong. It's not an animal at all. It's Agent D. Deadly's cleverly disguised 'dog bomb'. Hey – what's that ticking sound? If we were you, we'd turn the page RIGHT NOW!

DEADLY DICTIONARY

Agent – a very polite spy.

(See also Secret Agent – a spy who pretends to be tough but is secretly very polite.)

Assassinate – what comes after assassinseven and before assassinnine.

Bomb disposal – where bombs throw their rubbish.

CCTV – what you can't do do until you finish finish your homework.

Coldfinger – cousin of Goldfinger, but can't afford gloves.

Dr Maybe – cousin of Dr No, but much easier to persuade.

Enemy base – what you can hear when the enemy plays his stereo too loud.

Explosive – a plosive who's retired.

False name – what's written on the ID card of secret agent Fred False.

Getaway car – a rusty old banger that the garage managed to get away with selling to you.

Guided missile – a missile that is too old to be in the Brownies.

Hideout – what Dr Jekyll's other self says when he finishes chatting on his walkie-talkie.

Infrared – the colour spies turn when they get embarrassed.

Kung fu – self-defence method that involves leaping about.

Kung pu – what you might step in if you don't check where your dog's been before you start leaping about.

Lie detector – a special kind of knife used for filleting fish. OK, OK, it isn't. We lied.

(See also Fly detector – very useful when eating soup in the Spy School canteen.)

M – James Bond's boss and head of the Secret Service.

N – person who sat beside M at Spy School.

O – person who sat on the other side of M in Spy School and was always borrowing money.

P – didn't actually spend much time in Spy School as was always asking to go to the toilet.

Radar screen – where radars go to see their favourite films.

DID YOU HEAR ABOUT THE LETTER THAT FELL INTO THE CROCODILE PIT?

HE GOT ALPHA-BI

DID YOU HEAR ABOUT THE SPY WHO NICKED A DICTIONARY?

HE WAS BROUGHT TO BOOK.

Secret Service – what spies bring their cars to the garage for every six months.

Sharpshooter – a hedgehog with a pistol.

Silencer – sorry, can't tell you – someone might hear us.

Spy – something you do with your little eye.

Sty – something you get in your little eye if you do too much spying with it.

Torpedo – like ordinary dough, but a lot more likely to explode.

Undercover – where the pages of this book are.

Z – Another schoolmate of M's, but was always asleep in class.

CRIME TIME

As you travel the world on your top-secret business, be careful of genuine laws like these ones. They may sound strange but they're deadly serious ...

- Buying chewing gum is a crime in Singapore.
- In Montreal, Canada, it's illegal to swear in French.
- In Israel, you are not allowed to pick your nose on a Saturday.
- In Victoria, Australia, only a qualified electrician is allowed to change a light bulb.
- In Switzerland, you are not allowed to mow the lawn on a Sunday.
- It's against the law to wear a mask in Germany.
- In Italy, it's against the law for men to wear skirts.

With all the deadly stuff going on in this joke book, you'll need to make a quick getaway!

*Well, never fear – with our **super free gift** you'll be the most stylish secret agent on the whole block!*

*Simply turn the page for your own personal top-of-the-range **Supercharged Sports Car …***

NASTY NOTES

(Ssh! Stolen from Spy School's most secret files ...)

Dear Teacher

Thank you for pointing out to us that our son,
███████████████████ always hands in his
homework for Maths, English and ███████████
with bits blacked out. As we are both spies ourselves,
you can't blame our son for having grown up being a
bit suspicious. We promise this won't happen again and
if it does, you can contact us immediately at ████████
███████████

Yours sincerely
Mr and Mrs ████████████████

Dear Teacher

When we asked you if our daughter, Agent
XYZ, could change seats in the classroom, we
did not expect you to move her to one of
the ejector seats. Although we are very
pleased to hear that she is now top of the
class, we think it's high time you called the
fire brigade and got her down.

Best wishes
Mr and Mrs WXY

Dear Teacher

Regarding your complaint about our son, Agent
QED, you have only yourself to blame.
If you insist on giving your class lectures
on 'how not to give away secrets while being
interrogated', you can't very well blame him
for refusing to answer any questions in class
except for his name, rank and serial number.

Yours sincerely
Mr and Mrs ... actually, we're not going to
tell you our names, no matter what you do to
us.

NEXT TIME YOUR
PARENTS WRITE TO
ME, ASK THEM TO
POST IT LIKE
EVERYONE
ELSE!

Dear Teacher (again)

Further to our last letter about our son, Agent QED, not answering questions in class and your new complaint about him insulting you, we still think you have only yourself to blame. If you deliberately inject him with Truth Serum and then he tells you that you are a Baldy Old Trout, well, it's got to be the truth, hasn't it?

Yours sincerely
Mr and Mrs ... hah! Thought you could catch us out, eh? We're STILL not going to tell you that our surname is 'Brown', no matter what you do.

DEAR TEACHER

We are sorry that our daughter, Agent QXL, has not done her homework. She has had no time this week as she has had to spend all her time decoding the letter you sent home about her not doing her homework.
Yours sincerely
Mr & Mrs ... oh, we haven't got time to tell you.

Congratulations!

As you have done so well in surviving your reading of The World's Deadliest Joke Book, we have a special and very glamorous protection job for you:

You are assigned to protect

The World's Top CELEBRITY!

This is the job that all the world's top spies and secret agents have been fighting over, but YOU get to do it and your client is waiting overleaf ...

PRIVATE SPY

All the news we found out when nobody was looking

MAD SCIENTIST TAKES OVER WORLD!

Hundreds of secret agents rushed to the hideout of Dr Evil, the mad scientist who has just been released from jail, after hearing that he had taken over the world. Now Dr Evil is even madder. 'How do they expect me to go straight when as soon as they hear I've taken over my new shop, PIZZA WORLD, they turn up with tanks and frighten away my customers? The least they can do is use those tanks to help me deliver my pizzas. Mind you, that might scare my customers even more!'

SWIPED SECRETS STALL SHOW

A press conference was held today to announce the government's new plans to make it harder for spies to steal top-secret plans. At least, it SHOULD have been held today, but everyone had to be sent home because someone had stolen the plans.

SPOT THE BALL Competition

This week's competition has been cancelled thanks to Agent HJK who is very short-sighted and thought it was a 'shot the ball' competition. She turned up at the football pitch with a rocket launcher. Unfortunately, she is so short-sighted that she managed to miss the ball completely and launch herself into outer space, so we thought it was only fair to postpone the competition until she comes back down.

SHY SPY FOILS HAI GUY!

This year's World's Best Spy Award was taken home by Agent 004, an expert in disguise. The award was actually won by Agent 003, master of kung fu, but Agent 004 turned up to the award ceremony disguised as Agent 003 and took home the prize.

FIEND FAILS TO FIND FORTUNE

A huge reward has been offered to the first agent who can break into the secret hideout of international supervillain The CLAW. The reward has been offered by international supervillain The CLAW, who has lost his front door key. 'It's terrible,' he wailed. 'All my ill-gotten gains are inside and I can't get to them! And I'm afraid someone's going to nick them while I'm on the outside. There are a lot of nasty villains about these days, you know.'

STOP MEDAL-ING ABOUT!

Here's a quick peek into the Spy School medal cabinet, so you can see the great things some of our past pupils have achieved. Mind you, with all the deadly dangers they've had to deal with, it's no wonder they're past it!

Medal for Lion Taming

This was awarded to Agent H-34. All right, so the lions in question were actually SEA LIONS, but he did run the risk of getting slapped in the face with a wet fish!

Award for Keeping a Stiff Upper Lip

This was won by Agent K-68. She was actually competing for the 'Best Disguise' award but she accidentally put superglue on her false moustache.

Victoria Cross

Won by Agent 5-HJ when he forgot to collect his gran from Victoria Station as arranged. And if you don't think that's dangerous, you haven't seen his granny when she's cross.

Navigation Skills Certificate

This was awarded to Agent 78-HJ, or at least it should have been. Unfortunately, he lost his way and hasn't yet managed to find us so he can collect it.

CUT OUT AND PIN
TO LAPEL.

Medal for Coping
with Great Pain

This was given to Agent KB4. She wasn't
sure why she'd got it and then she realized
the medal has a really sharp pin.

Medal for Coping
with Even Greater Pain

Congratulations! This medal's been
awarded to YOU for making it through
The World's Deadliest Joke Book!

AN ESSENTIAL ITEM IN EVERY SECRET AGENT'S KIT:

THE WORLD'S MOST EFFECTIVE

BULLETPROOF VEST!

You've tried the rest, now try the best! Guaranteed to protect you morning, noon and night!

STOP PRESS: Due to an unfortunate misprint in the above ad, 'bulletproof vest' should actually have read 'BALLET-proof vest' – in other words, a vest that you can pull over your head to avoid having to watch really boring ballet. If you have already sent money for the vest, we will, of course, send it straight back. If you have already received your vest and have tried to use it to stop bullets, we'll keep the money, thanks – after all, YOU certainly won't have any further use for it.

**Tired of your ordinary old auto?
Crazy about clever contraptions?
No self-respecting spy should be seen in
anything other than ...**

The XZZL007 SPECTACULAR SECRET AGENT CAR!

Let's face it, the last thing a secret agent needs a car for is to get from place to place.
As every master spy knows, what's really important about a super secret agent car is all those hidden little gimmicks and surprises, such as:

**Colour-changing paintwork for disguise!
Instant oil slick to shake off pursuers!
Explosive device hidden under the bonnet!**

Ask for a test drive today – you'll never look back!

Ahem ... it has been pointed out that our hidden gimmicks and surprises aren't so much because this car is a super secret-agent model as because it's a horrible old banger with dodgy spray painting, a leaky fuel tank and an engine that's liable to blow up at any minute, so we'd better make a quick getaway with your cash. Or at least we would if our car would start ...

Mucked up a mission? Made an ass of yourself on an assignment?

Don't worry about looking like the stupidest spy in the secret service.

Now you can return to base with a smile on your face because on the next page you'll find that agents from The World's Deadliest Joke Book have done your dirty work for you.

Yes, at great personal risk we've stolen a copy of one of the spy world's top SECRET FORMULAS and we're going to give it to you, free.

For your eyes only, turn the page to view the secret formula for
The World's Best Invisible Ink.

I SPY A BIG LIE

An essential spy skill is being able to tell the truth from fiction. Can you search through the deadly facts in this section and decide which one is a fake?

The total number of cars in Britain in 1894 was two.

In 1530, a cook was boiled to death for poisoning two members of his master's family.

I NEED A NEW BEDROOM FOR MY DOLL... SHE EXPLODED AND DESTROYED THE OLD ONE.

TOYS

The Barbie doll was designed by a man who also designed explosive missiles.

In 1910, strongman Rama Naidu allowed a fully grown elephant to stand on him.

The most poisonous scorpions are found in Tunisia.

The poison arrow frog is the deadliest frog in the world.

I'M A POISONOUS FROG.. COME NEAR ME AND YOU'LL CROAK.

Tarantulas can live to be thirty years old.

DID YOU SPOT THE FALSE FACT?
It was the one on the previous page saying that one of these facts was a fake.

87

Have you got these top-secret tomes on your bookshelf?

Explosive Devices by Dynah Mite

SPY HAIRSTYLES BY JAMES BLONDE

Unarmed Combat by K. Ratty

Armed Combat by Tommy Gunn

See Where All That Combat Gets You? by D. Ceased

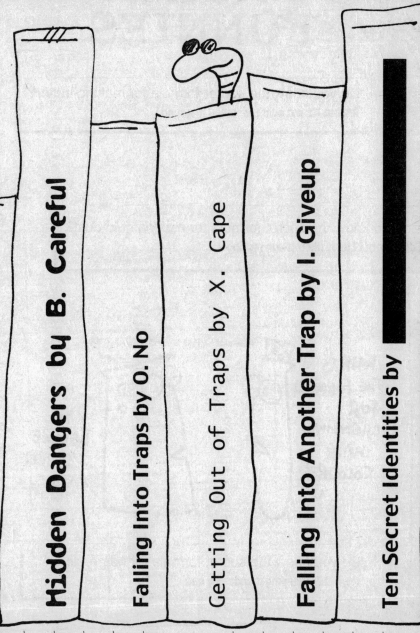

Hidden Dangers by B. Careful

Falling Into Traps by O. No

Getting Out of Traps by X. Cape

Falling Into Another Trap by I. Giveup

Ten Secret Identities by

FORMULA FUNNIES

'Do you know the secret formula for making butter?'
'Yes, but I'm not going to spread it around.'

'Do you know the secret formula for making gold dust?'
'I used to, but I let it slip through my fingers.'

WHAT'S THE FORMULA FOR CHANGING HAIR COLOUR?

I'D DYE BEFORE I'D TELL YOU...

'Do you know the secret formula for hair restorer?'
'Yes, but I'm keeping it under my hat.'

'Do you know the secret formula for mummification?'
'Yes, but I'm keeping it under wraps.'

'Do you know the secret formula for nuclear power?'
'Yes, and it gives me a very warm glow.'

DO YOU KNOW THE FORMULA FOR HEDGEHOG PAPER?

YES, BUT IT'S VERY HARD TO GRASP!

'Do you know the secret formula for making very sharp knives?'
'No, but I could make a very good stab at it.'

'Do you know the secret formula for making dentures out of glue?'
'Yes, but I'm staying tight-lipped.'

I SPY

First Spy: Why have you glued
two humps on your back?
Second Spy: Ssh! It's camel-flage.

First Spy: That book on self defence you lent me really works.

Second Spy: How is that?

First Spy: Whenever someone attacks me, I hit them over the head with it.

GREAT!
OPEN IT
THEN!

DEADLY
JOKE FILE #2

Spy Teacher: What do you get if you type 'zyxwvutsrqponmlkjihgfedcba' into your decoder?
Spy Pupil: Very sore fingers.

I'M NOT MUCH GOOD AT DISGUISES THOUGH... FOR SOME REASON EVERYONE 'NOSE' IT'S ME!

Why is Pinocchio good at spying?
Because it's hard to get him to come out of the woodwork.

'I've got to stop using these
infrared goggles – I'm getting
spots in front of my eyes.'
'Have you seen an optician?'
'No, just spots.'

'Doctor, Doctor, my little brother
thinks he's a bazooka.'
**'Well, bring him in so I can
cure him.'**
'I can't! Every time I go near
him he shoots out the window.'

Spy Pupil: Sorry I'm late for school. I dreamed I was swimming through shark-infested waters.
Spy Teacher: How could that make you late for school?
Spy Pupil: I lost my trunks so I couldn't wake up until there was nobody looking.

I LIKE JOKES I CAN GET MY TEETH INTO...

'The Stunt Driving teacher did three laps of the Spy School car park, jumped over fourteen traffic cones and then skidded to a perfect stop.'
'Why weren't the pupils impressed?'
'Because he wasn't in his car at the time.'

I COULD DO WITH A JOKE TO STOP ME ENDING UP 'DOWN IN THE MOUTH'..

Explorer: I'm a bit worried about our trip to the jungle – it's a very scary place.
Guide: Don't worry. In all my jungle trips, I've only once failed to bring everyone back alive.
Explorer: Oh good. How many trips have you done?
Guide: This is my second.

'I'm a master of tongue fu.'
'Don't you mean kung fu?'
'No, I just talk my way out of trouble.'

SPY SCHOOL NOTICEBOARD

WARNING:

Please don't run in the school corridors as this is very dangerous (unless, of course, you ask one of the pupils in stunt class to do your running for you).

Football Fixtures:

All football matches have been cancelled so that the pitch can be re-laid after last week's embarrassing incident. The school team is reminded that having a 'good strong defence' doesn't necessarily have to involve a Sherman tank.

Special note for pupils in code-breaking class:

Fdk jreuire lfksdhv ;kldsk; ;joj;l;liio[psd trpri Gjkglgl jkjl; ;lj;so oksjlhlh ;'k;kk'ks ';k;'k Jflkjljl;jls ;k;k;'k'wehp'ret[ha[]pb Edl][l[]l[[
(This isn't actually in code, it's just that the teacher's computer is on the blink.)

98

PETS' DAY
If any young agents have been issued with robot dogs, could you please ensure that they are house-trained before bringing them to Pets' Day. The puddles of oil all over the school are making us break our necks!

I NEED TO PUT A NOTICE UP... I'VE LOST MY DOG!

WHAT NAME DOES IT ANSWER TO?

IT'S A SPY DOG — IT DOESN'T ANSWER QUESTIONS, EVEN UNDER INTERROGATION!

TNT

<u>Pupils Must Not Smoke Behind the Bicycle Sheds!</u>
In future, blow the smoke away from your rocket launcher as soon as you finish using it!

Bomb-disposal Demonstration
Mr Englebert Einstein, our Physics teacher, will be giving another talk and demonstration on bomb disposal – just like the one he gave last year. If you'd like to take part, go and have a word with him. You will find him in Classroom 3D (also in Classrooms 2F, 4A and in several parts of the playing field).

SCHOOL TRIP
This year's school trip will be to a top-secret location. If anyone knows where, could you please tell the headmaster as he can't organize the trip until he finds out.

HOW DID YOU GET ALL THOSE INJURIES ON YOUR SCHOOL TRIP?

WHEN I TRIPPED – I WAS – CARRYING OUR HAND-GRENADE SUPPLIES!

CLASSIFIED CRACKS

'Doctor, Doctor, I keep
thinking I'm a double agent.'
**'Well, come and see me next
Wednesday and Thursday.'**

First Spy: Are you a better shot
with your left hand or your right hand?
Second Spy: My right hand.
First Spy: And what about when you
use a gun?

Why did the supervillain throw
custard and jelly at the spy?
He was just trifling with him.

HOW DID
THE ENEMY
AGENTS GET
YOU TO REVEAL
ALL YOUR
SECRETS?

Spy Teacher: Have you read the
book on how to avoid being
hypnotized?
**Spy Pupil: Yes, but it put me
to sleep.**

I THINK THEY USED
HIPPO-NOSIS!

Knock, knock.
Who's there?
Gun.
Gun who?
**Gun to stand here all day
until you open the door.**

Why did the explorer throw his camera
into the crocodile-infested river?
He wanted lots of snaps.

HOW DO
SKELETONS
RELAX?

Why aren't skeletons good in
dangerous situations?
They are very easily rattled.

WITH A SKULL
AND CROSSWORD - BONES.

Why did the knife
thrower have bags
under his eyes?
**Because he was working
the knife shift.**

'Have you seen the high fence they've
built around Spy School?'
'Yes, I just can't get over it.'
'Oh, but in the middle of the high fence
there's a very low gate.'
**'Aha! That's something they've
overlooked!'**

Spy Teacher: Have you read the
book on dynamite?
**Spy Pupil: Yes, it really blew
my mind.**

First Spy Teacher: Did your pupils enjoy your lecture on how to escape?
Second Spy Teacher: I don't know. When I turned to write on the board they disappeared.

Why did the secret agent pour tomato sauce all over his car?
So his enemies couldn't ketchup with him.

WHY WAS THE SECRET AGENT TOMATO ALWAYS IN DANGER?

Why was the spy spinning round and round?
Because he had a top secret.

'Spy to Headquarters – help! The enemy has me by the throat!'
'Are you choking?'
'No, I'm serious.'

'What's the difference between a red button and a green button?'
'I don't know.'
'Well, I'm not letting YOU defuse any bombs then!'

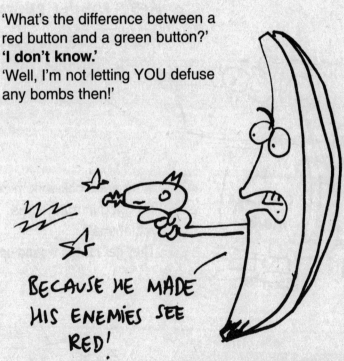

BECAUSE HE MADE HIS ENEMIES SEE RED!

Have you heard about the two enemy spies who got married?
It was love at first fight.

What do detectives drink at
break time?
Cop-uccinos.

THEY CAN NEVER
KEEP ME IN PRISON
COS I'VE GOT MY
OWN KEY!

CLOCKWORK
MOUSE

Why are clockwork mice
no good in dangerous
situations?
They get far too wound up.

'Doctor, Doctor, I keep
thinking I'm a killer
octopus.'
'Oh, get a grip on yourself.'

What's a secret agent's favourite
Italian food?
Spy-ghetti.

IF THERE'S ONE THING
WE SPY CHEFS LIKE
IT'S PUTTING ALL THE
PIZZAS OF A PUZZLE
TOGETHER!

'When Spy School pupils
come through security,
do they have to be
checked?'
'No, they can be any pattern
they like.'

How do secret agents
stop time running out?
They hide its trainers.

What do DJs play at the supervillains' disco?
Criminal records.

GOSH! WHERE DID YOU FIND THOSE SECRET PLANS?

Where do elephant spies carry secret papers?
Hidden in their trunks.

AT A JUMBO SALE!

How do ghost spies see through walls?
With X-ray spooktacles.

'Have you heard about the spy chef who had a radio that looked like a piece of bacon?'
'Really? Did it work very well?'
'No, there was far too much crackling.'

Why did the bomb-disposal expert carry herbs in his pocket?
In case he needed a little more thyme.

WHY DO HAMBURGERS MAKE TERRIBLE SECRET AGENTS!

THEY CAN'T CUT THE MUSTARD.

SHAKE

What do secret agents eat with their hamburgers?
French spies.

'Doctor, Doctor, I keep thinking I'm
a spy. Can you help me?'
**'Of course I can – but first stop
breaking into my filing cabinet.'**

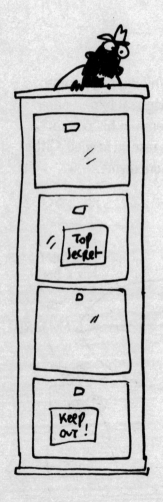

WHERE DO SPIES KEEP
INFORMATION ON
BEANSTALKS?

'Doctor, Doctor, I'm so
big I can't fit at my
computer terminal.'
'Have you tried to diet?'
'Yes, but no matter what
colour it is, I still can't fit.'

IN A FEE-FILE-FO-
FUM.

How do ghostly spies sneak into buildings?
They use their skeleton keys.

WHY DID THE SPY FILL THE PHONEBOX WITH INSECTS?

HE WANTED TO BUG THE LINES.

Which secret agent swings around on a web?
Spy-derman.

What do stunt drivers do at weekends?
Stay home and just crash.

What do you get if you cross
spies with cowboys?
The Magnificent 007.

'Waiter, there's a banana skin
in my soup!'
**'Yes, sir. Someone's trying to slip
something into your drink.'**

WHAT DID THE
SPY SAY WHEN
HE CAPTURED
THE BANANA?

How do bomb-disposal
experts dance?
Slow, slow, tick, tick, slow.

Why doesn't Indiana Jones
like crashing cars?
Because he might get whiplash.

What do elephants do
whenever danger threatens?
Elefaint.

I WANT YOU TO
TELL ME THE FRUIT,
THE WHOLE
FRUIT AND
NOTHING BUT THE
FRUIT!

First Spy: If I were in trouble,
would you save me?
**Second Spy: Of course I would. I'd
save you the trouble of calling me
by running away.**

Why are matchstick men
no good in a crisis?
**Because they're way too hot-
headed.**

WHERE DO SPY
SALMON WEAR
THEIR SECRET
DECODING RINGS?

What's another name for a
lecture on bomb disposal?
A tick talk.

Why don't salmon make
good double agents?
**People always smell
something fishy.**

ON THEIR FISH
FINGERS!

Why are vampires no good
when there's danger?
They always get in a flap.

WHY ARE VAMPIRE
BATS GOOD IN A
CRISIS?

Spy School Teacher: Is quick
decision-making the mark of a
good spy?
Spy School Pupil: Yes and no.

'COS THEY KNOW
HOW TO WING IT!

Why did the policeman have
a twig in his ear?
**Because he was in Special
Branch.**

TNT

Why do hens make very good
detectives?
**Because they're good at spotting
fowl play.**

Why is the invisible man no
good in a crisis?
**Whenever there's danger, he
disappears.**

WHY WAS
THE INVISIBLE
SPY NO GOOD AT
DISGUISES?

EVERYONE
COULD SEE
THROUGH HIM!

Why did the supervillain
strap a cake into his
electric chair?
Because it was a current cake.

Why do supervillains always
have to borrow money?
Because crime doesn't pay.

GO AWAY— I'M
READING MY
MYSTERY NOVEL...

Why did the spy sit in
the fridge?
He wanted to keep his cool.

IT'S A REAL
CHILLER!

FRIDGE

Where do supervillains do
house cleaning?
At the scene of the grime.

What happened when the dish and spoon spied on the cat?
They discovered that she was on the fiddle.

How did the cow feel when they told her?
Like she'd been hey diddle diddled.

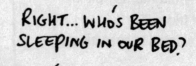

RIGHT... WHO'S BEEN SLEEPING IN OUR BED?

What's the first thing the Three Bears did at Spy School?
They learned to pick Goldi-locks.

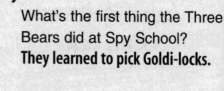

I'M NOT TELLING YOU... I'M TRAINED TO BEAR UP UNDER PRESSURE.

'Doctor, Doctor, I keep thinking
I'm a gun.'
'Well, shoot over here immediately.'

WHAT DID
THE COLONEL
SKUNK SAY
TO THE
PRIVATE
SKUNK?

How do underwater
detectives catch crooks?
They look for fish fingerprints.

STOP
DISOBEYING
ODOURS.

Why did the skunk wear a
disguise?
To put enemies off the scent.

Spy School Teacher: So what would you do if you were trapped in quicksand?
Spy School Pupil: I don't know, sir.
Spy School Teacher: But I told you in class yesterday.
Spy School Pupil: I know, but it hasn't sunk in yet.

WHY DO SPY CHICKENS MESS UP DANGEROUS SITUATIONS?

First Spy: I sent a letter to my mum yesterday.
Second Spy: Was it in code?
First Spy: No – in an envelope.

What do you say to a double
agent on his birthday?
'Many happy U-turns.'

Did you hear about the
killer chicken?
**She was an assault and
battery hen.**

Why was the spy dancing
on top of the telephone?
**He'd been ordered to tap all
the calls.**

What did one fuse say to
the other fuse?
'Let's go out together.'

What's green and scaly and
carries a machine gun?
The Loch Ness Mobster.

YOU TAKE THE
HIGH ROAD, I'LL
TAKE THE LOW
ROAD...

Which supervillain lives in the
sewers?
The Great Drain Robber.

What do you get if you cross
Shakespeare with a secret
agent?
Rome007 and Juliet.

What do you find on top
of a skunk bomb?
The phews.

YOU CAN
TAKE WHATEVER
ROAD YOU LIKE—
I'M OFF BEFORE THE
LOCH NESS MOBSTER
GETS ME!

Why did the soldier have a
budgie in his rucksack?
**Because he was a parrot-
trooper.**

What do you get if you
cross a supervillain with
a wizard?
Harry Rotter.

WHY SHOULD
YOU NEVER TRY
TO BREAK INTO
A CONVENT?

WHACK!!

How do mummies run
from danger?
Wrapidly.

Why are musicians good in a fight?
Because they can stand the sight of violins.

How do nuns get fit enough to handle danger?
They do hymnastics.

BECAUSE EVERYBODY THERE KNOWS ¡OUCH¡ NUN FU!

What did the giant secret agent say?
'Fee-spie-fo-fum.'

Why is Quasimodo good at disguises?
Because whoever he tries to be, he's sure to be a ringer.

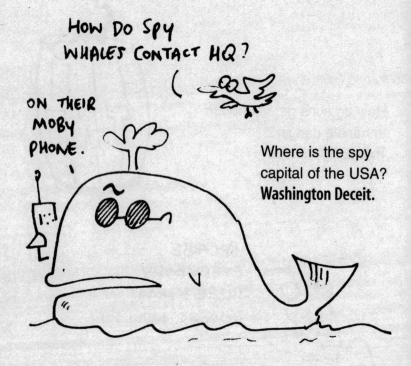

HOW DO SPY WHALES CONTACT HQ?

ON THEIR MOBY PHONE.

Where is the spy capital of the USA?
Washington Deceit.

What do you get if you cross a whale with a pistol?
A very tired arm.

Spy Teacher: You've been sending
other pupils coded messages
saying that I'm stupid!
**Spy Pupil: Well, I knew you'd
want it kept a secret!**

Explorer: Why are you rubbing
toothpaste all over yourself?
Guide: To keep tigers away.
Explorer: But this is Africa –
there aren't any tigers.
Guide: See? It works, doesn't it?

Careers Teacher: I think you'd be
best at spying underwater.
Spy Pupil: Why do you say that?
Careers Teacher: Because all your
marks are below C level.

WHY SHOULD YOU BRIEF
FROGMEN TWICE ABOUT
SPY
MISSIONS?

Careers Teacher: I think you'd
make a great stuntman.
Spy Pupil: Why's that?
Careers Teacher: Because I wish
you'd go and take a running
jump at yourself.

'Dad – do you like mystery stories?'
'Yes, why?'
'Because I've torn the last page
out of your spy novel.'

BECAUSE THEY'RE
VERY FROG-ETFUL!

Why can't Spy School
have its own web site?
**Nobody will give away the
password.**

Why did the captured spy ask for
a cake with a ruler inside it?
To see how long he's spent in prison.

Why couldn't the
stunt-driving student
do his homework?
His computer crashed.

Have you heard about the spy
who spent all night trying to
decode a secret message?
Eventually it dawned on him.

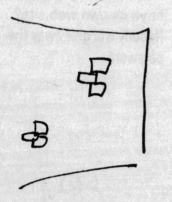

Why did James Bond put a clock
on his ejector seat?
He wanted to raise the alarm.

What is the
stuntman's favourite
type of tea?
Casual-tea.

HA! YOU MIGHT HAVE
PUSHED ME OFF THE
WALL... BUT I DID A
TRIPLE BACK FLIP AND
LANDED ON MY FEET!

Why do eggs make bad secret
agents?
Because they crack under pressure.

KING'S HORSE
H.Q.

LOOK!
IT'S
HUMPTY —
STUNT-Y!

'Doctor, Doctor, I think I'm a secret agent.'
'How long have you felt like this?'
'I'm sorry, I can't give away classified
information.'

Why did Harry Potter study
martial arts?
In case he got muggled.

Why did the spy go to
the cinema?
To see a microfilm.

WHAT DID
ONE SPY
CAT SAY
TO THE
OTHER
SPY
CAT?

'Doctor, Doctor, I keep thinking
I'm a bomb.'
**'Sorry, I'm a bit busy at the
moment.'**
'Fine, I'll just go off, then.'

Spy One: Why are you so sad?
Spy Two: Last night I sent myself a coded message and now I don't know who it's from.

DON'T LOOK NOW, BUT I THINK WE'RE BEING TAILED!

Secret Agent: Every time I come back from a mission my legs ache.
Doctor: That's just age.
Secret Agent: But my arms are just as old and they don't ache at all.

'My dog just passed his code-
breaking exams.'
'What an intelligent animal!'
'Not really – the cat always has
to help him with his homework.'

QUICK!
LET'S TUNNEL
OUT OF THIS
DANGEROUS
BOOK!

Supervillain: I hear James Bond was
giving you trouble while you were
questioning him.
**Henchman: It's not the questioning
I had trouble with. It's just that he
wouldn't give me any answers.**

Spy Teacher: Did you read that book I told you to on how to open locked doors?
Spy Pupil: Yes, but I found it very difficult to get into.

NOW THAT'S AN IDEA I CAN REALLY DIG!

Spy Pupil: I thought the headmaster was going to give us a talk on escapology?
Spy Teacher: I know, but he's a bit tied up at the moment.

Spy Pupil: Sir, what's the best way of preventing an enemy from sneaking up on you?
Spy Teacher: Always walk around backwards.

I'M AN EXPERT ON THICKBOXING...

DON'T YOU MEAN 'KICKBOXING?'

First Spy Pupil: How was Boxing class today?
Second Spy Pupil: It really knocked me out.

NO I MEAN 'THICKBOXING'- I KEEP STUBBING MY TOE!

Why doesn't Santa like being
locked up by evil villains?
Because he's Claus-trophobic.

What do you get if
you lend James
Bond a tenner?
A spy-o-u.

Why should you never add baked
beans to a secret formula?
Someone might get wind of it.

WHAT DO SPIES
DO WHEN THEIR
GETAWAY BOAT
SINKS?

BRING
ON A
SUB.

Which Teletubby is an
underwater swimmer?
Deepsea.

How do very short spies
keep in contact?
By wee mail.

Why do wasps like danger?
They get a buzz out of it.

What do werewolves shout on
the shooting range?
'Ready, aim, fur!'

What did the spy say when he was
chased by a gorilla?
'I'll chimpanzee you later.'

Why does James Bond wear a
black tuxedo?
**If he wore a polka-dot tuxedo, he'd be
too easy to spot.**

Spy Teacher: For your
homework I want you
to write an essay
entitled 'Alertness and
how it can save you'.
**Pupil: Could you
repeat that? I wasn't
listening the first
time.**

WHO ARE THE COOLEST
SPIES IN THE BUSINESS?

THE ONES FROM
M.I. HIGH 5!

First Detective: I've been on a case all night.
Second Detective: Don't you think you'd be more comfortable on a bed like everyone else?

'Why did you throw your computer into the bath?'
'The plumber told me it needed a new plug.'

HOW DOES A SPY'S COMPUTER KEEP SECRETS?

BY KEEPING ITS MOUSE SHUT!

Why are pigs no good at sharpshooting?
They keep running out of ham-unition.

First Spy Pupil: I hear your class had a lecture on surviving earthquakes.
Second Spy Pupil: Yes – but it was no great shakes.

OOPS! I'VE ACCIDENTALLY HIT THE SPY SCHOOL AMMO DUMP!

Weapons Teacher: Can you remember how to use a boomerang?
Spy Pupil: Not now, but I'm sure it will come back to me.

Spy Teacher: That was a good essay you wrote on the dangers of quicksand.
Spy Pupil: Yes, I really got stuck in.

UH-OH..
NOW I'M
REALLY
A BOOM-ERANG!

How do secret agents learn their vowels?
A-e-spy-o-u mail.

Why did the secret agent fill his car with old newspapers?
He wanted to tear down the road.

'Doctor, Doctor, I keep thinking
I'm a double agent.'
'What's causing that?'
'I'm in two minds.'

WHERE SHOULD YOU
SEND A BATTERED
VIKING?

How do Vikings send
secret messages?
By Norse code.

What do explosives
experts do at 11 a.m.?
Take a TNT break.

What do rival spies do
when they have to divide
up a birthday cake?
They hold piece negotiations.

Where do secret
agents go sailing?
On the Spy-tanic.

Why did the assassin cut five
centimetres off his knife?
He wanted to try a short cut.

What do you call a spy who
steals giant telescopes?
A Hubble agent.

Which Lord Mayor
of London had lots
of secret gadgets?
Trick Whittington.

WHAT SOUND DOES
A BOMB MAKE
WHEN IT'S
ON THE
MOON?

What do you get if you
cross a currant pudding
with a master of disguise?
Never Spotted Dick.

How did the spy break into the
Three Bears' house?
He picked the Goldilocks.

IT LUNAR-TICKS!

'Doctor, Doctor, I keep thinking
I'm an ejector seat.'
**'Was this something you
expected?'**
'No, it just sprung up on me.'

What do secret agents suck
on in the cinema?
Ejector sweets.

What do you get if you cross a
dangerous barbarian with an ice
cream?
Vanilla the Hun.

Why did the policeman put ice cream in the middle of the motorway?
Someone had told him to put out some cones.

Why did the security guard paint his barrier with black and white squares?
Because it was a checkpoint.

Which Dwarf put up the best fight?
Bash-ful.

WHAT SONG DO KARATE DWARFS SING?

Who beat up the
Seven Dwarfs?
Snow Fight.

HAiii-HO!

Why wouldn't Mr Wonka
work in the Deadly
Chocolate Factory?
It gave him the Willies.

What's yellow, has lots of teeth
and is very dangerous if you're
crossing a river?
A pirah-nana.

Who did the codebreaker send
a Mother's Day card to?
His enig-Ma.

THE WORLD'S DEADLIEST READERS!

When Puffin ran a deadly joke competition on their web site, they were expecting some pretty lethal entries. But the jokes you sent in were so fatally bad even our celebrity judge, Dr Evil, couldn't carry on. He was last seen running out of the building, screaming 'Please, no more!' Here are the jokes that tortured him the most ...

READERS! THESE JOKES ARE AWFUL! FAR WORSE THEN ANYTHING I COULD COME UP WITH...

What do you call James Bond in the bath?
Bubble-O-Seven.

James Buckle, Solihull

What has eight legs and catches criminals?
A spy-der.

Calum Walker, Durham

Two men dressed in armour go to a hotel and ask 'Have you a room for two knights?'

Adam Calvert, Pudsey

IN OTHER WORDS, I'M SO PROUD OF YOU!

What do you call a secret agent who interrogates his enemies?
Question Mark.

Katy Fryd, Nelson

To find out how to send one of your jokes to Puffin, take a look at our web site: www.puffin.co.uk

155